A PLACE TO START A FAMILY

Poems About Creatures That Build

David L. Harrison • Illustrated by **Giles Laroche**

Charlesbridge

With all my love to my wife, Sandy, who is always there
—D. L. H.

For the Nature Conservancy, which helps to protect and conserve
the habitats where many of these animal structures are built
—G. L.

Published by Charlesbridge
85 Main Street
Watertown, MA 02472
(617) 926-0329
www.charlesbridge.com

Library of Congress Cataloging-in-Publication Data
Names: Harrison, David L. (David Lee), 1937– author.
    Laroche, Giles, illustrator.
Title: A place to start a family: poems about creatures that build /
    David L. Harrison; illustrated by Giles Laroche.
Description: Watertown, MA: Charlesbridge, [2018]
Identifiers: LCCN 2016053964 (print) LCCN 2017009817 (ebook)
    ISBN 9781580897488 (reinforced for library use)
    ISBN 9781632896056 (ebook)
    ISBN 9781632896063 (ebook pdf)
Subjects: LCSH: Animals—Habitations—Juvenile literature.
    Children's poetry, American.
Classification: LCC QL756 .H35925 2018 (print)
    LCC QL756 (ebook) DDC 591.56/4—dc23
LC record available at https://lccn.loc.gov/2016053964

Printed in China
(hc) 10 9 8 7 6 5 4 3 2 1

Illustrations done in cut-paper relief on a variety of
    hand-painted papers
Display type set in Mikado by Hannes Von Doehren
Text type set in Triplex by Emigre Graphics
Photographs by 5000K Color Studio, Pembroke, MA
Color separations by Colourscan Print Co Pte Ltd, Singapore
Printed by 1010 Printing International Limited
    in Huizhou, Guangdong, China
Production supervision by Brian G. Walker
Designed by Sarah Richards Taylor

CREATURES THAT BUILD

For thousands of years people have built shelters to live in and protect their families. We use wood, cloth, brick, concrete, steel, glass, and more to create safe and unique homes. Many animals are builders, too. They use materials they can find, such as dirt, leaves, grass, twigs, tree limbs, shells, fur, hair, clay, and sand.

Some make their own building materials. Spiders spin their own thread. Stickleback fish make their own glue. Paper wasps make their own paper. Some animals live in their structures and some don't, and they all need a place to start a family. Turn the page to meet some of nature's most interesting architects and learn how they build!

BUILDERS UNDERGROUND

Black-Tailed Prairie Dog

Young ones kiss,
play king of the hill,
chirp and trill,
voices shrill.

Adults tunnel
towns below,
somehow know
where chambers go.

They line the nursery
with care,
decide where
to hide their lair.

Mothers guard
while babies sleep,
stretch and creep,
warm and deep.

Star-Nosed Mole

You never know
where I might hide.
Secret tunnels
lead outside,
sometimes beneath
a ledge or limb,
sometimes I even
have to swim.

I keep my babies
safe and dry,
but otherwise
I don't deny—
I love it wet
and full of bugs,
worms, beetles,
grubs, and slugs.

It's even better
in the bogs,
crunching fish
and munching frogs.
Don't have to see
to find my share.
It's my nose
that gets me there.

California Trapdoor Spider

In a silk-lined hole
she lies in wait,
patiently,
to seal the fate
of cricket,
centipede,
or roach. . . .

Eyes
watch the prey
approach. . . .

She lifts the door,
leaps,
and *zap!*
Another
victim
down
the
trap.

And in the dark,
without a sound,
her hungry babies
gather around.

BUILDERS ON LAND

King Cobra

Twisting
and coiling,
you use
your own
body and
    magically manage,
        with no arms or legs,
            to craft a tight cover
                from layers and layers
                    of leaves
                    you have carried
                to protect your eggs.
            No other serpent
      can master
        this test.
            No other serpent
                can fashion
                    a nest.

Termite

The queen is busy laying eggs.
It's what she does the best.
Soldiers prowl the darkened halls
as they protect the nest.
Of all the termite jobs to do,
workers do the rest.

Workers look for woody food.
It's a job they do the best.
And they groom the colony
to keep a tidy nest.
Queens lay and soldiers guard.
Workers do the rest.

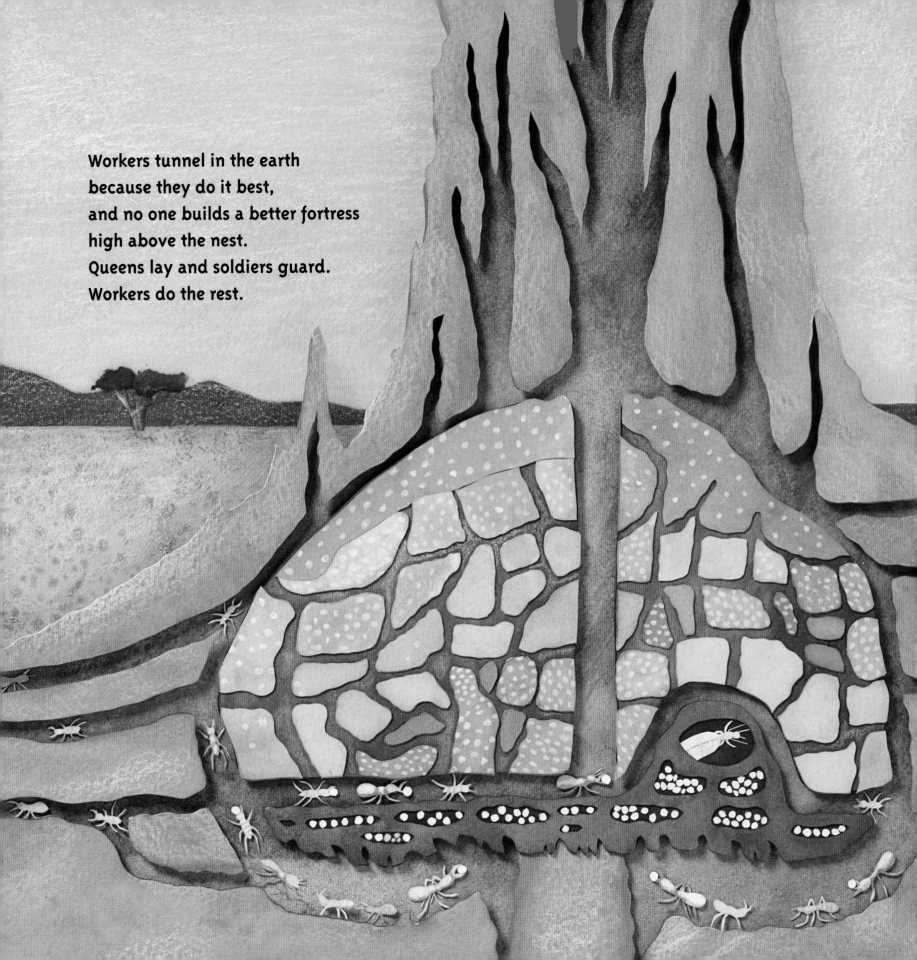

Workers tunnel in the earth
because they do it best,
and no one builds a better fortress
high above the nest.
Queens lay and soldiers guard.
Workers do the rest.

Yellow Garden Spider

You throw a line of silken thread
   and let it flutter where it will,
   to catch on limb or windowsill,
   then use your ancient weaver's skill
to make it hold you when you tread.

Back and forth you bridge the gap,
   spinning out the thread to sew,
   crafting in the dark you go,
   putting on your magic show,
creating your artistic trap.

Now to build your strength you wait
till fragile moth or careless fly
has bad luck to blunder by
so you can greet it eye to eye
and at your leisure seal its fate.

And when the tiny eggs you guard
hatch, as baby spiders must,
spiderlings the size of dust
sail away on gentle gust
to decorate another yard.

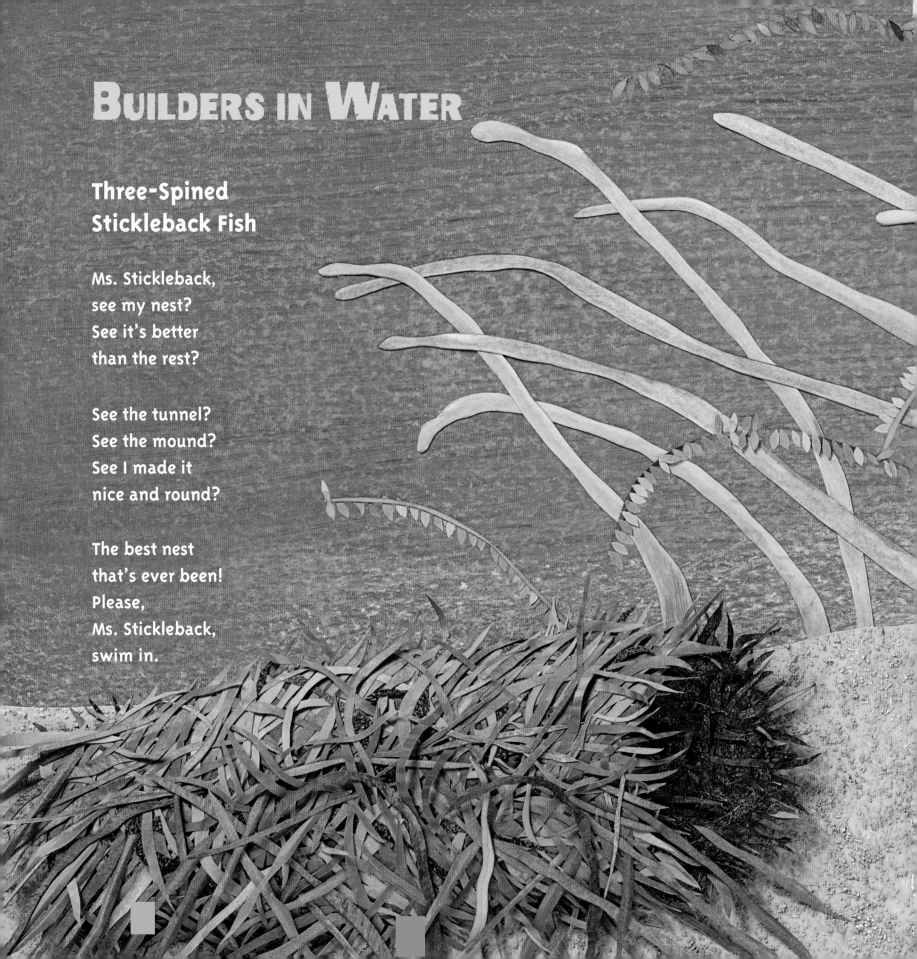

BUILDERS IN WATER

Three-Spined Stickleback Fish

Ms. Stickleback,
see my nest?
See it's better
than the rest?

See the tunnel?
See the mound?
See I made it
nice and round?

The best nest
that's ever been!
Please,
Ms. Stickleback,
swim in.

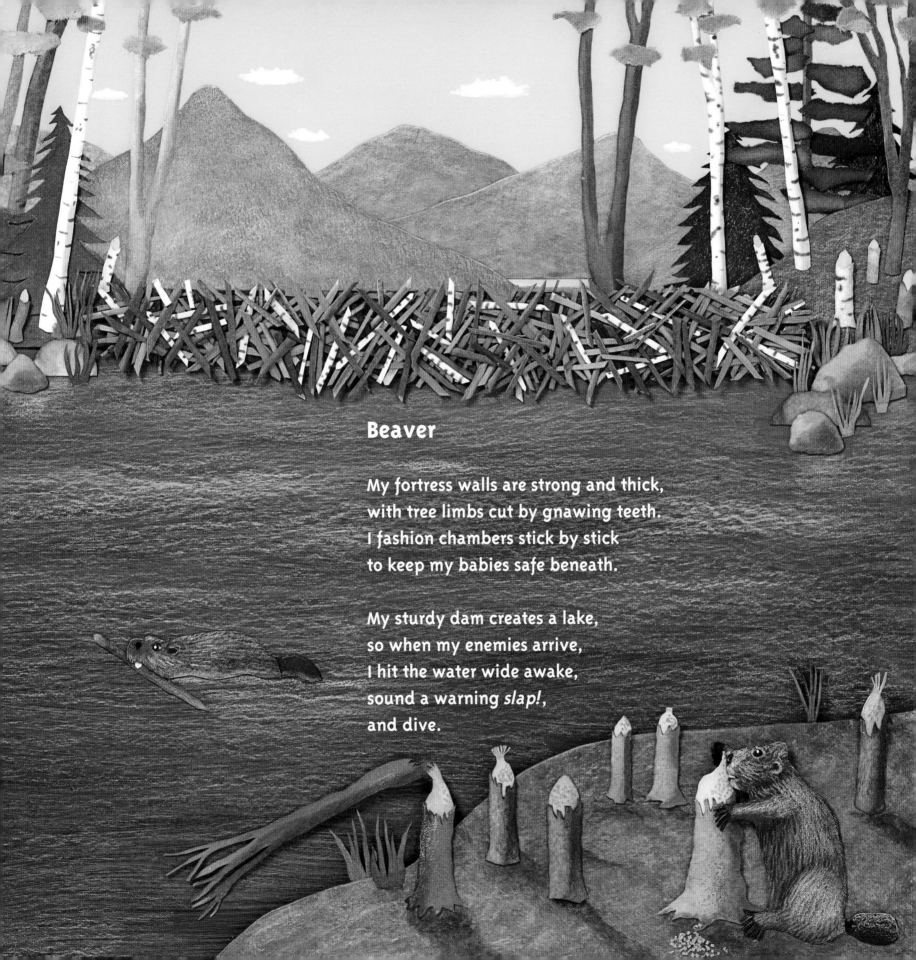

Beaver

My fortress walls are strong and thick,
with tree limbs cut by gnawing teeth.
I fashion chambers stick by stick
to keep my babies safe beneath.

My sturdy dam creates a lake,
so when my enemies arrive,
I hit the water wide awake,
sound a warning *slap!*,
and dive.

White-Spotted Pufferfish

Tiny sculptor
thinks grand,
builds a nest
out of sand
forty times
his own size,
trying to
attract a prize.

With tail and fin,
hoping he
will soon charm
a willing she,
he works hard
day and night.

Will he win
a mate?

He might.

BUILDERS IN AIR

Red Ovenbird

How do you hide
your nest
like that?

Protect your chicks
inside
like that?

How do you know
to weave
like that?

With grass and hair
and leaves
like that?

Make it round
with twigs
like that?

On the ground
or limb
like that?

We're so glad
you sing
like that.

And make the forest
ring
like that!

White Stork

When high on chimney top you nest,
legend tells us those who dwell
within the house are surely blessed.

How old your nest no one can tell,
you keep it in such good repair.
Your ancestors placed it well.

With sturdy sticks they built it there,
where now you cast your lucky spell
and raise your baby storks with care.

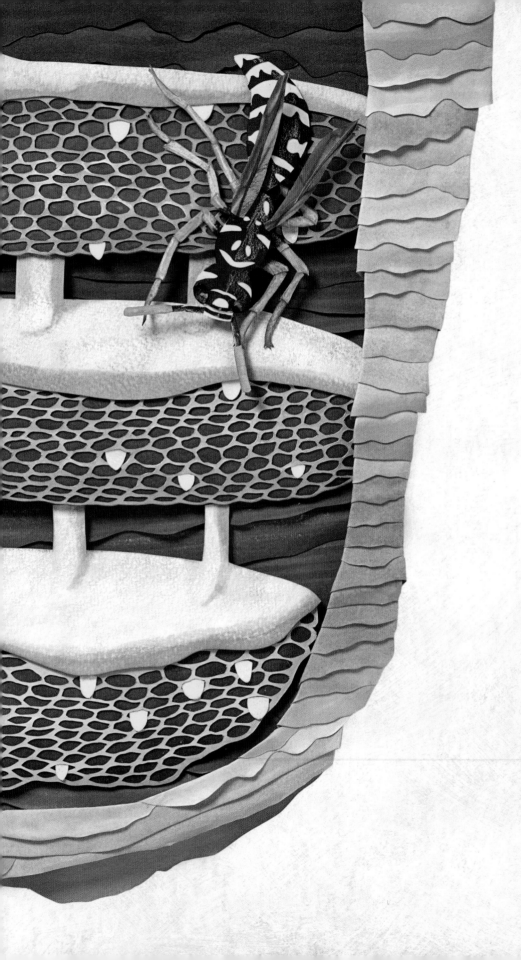

European Paper Wasp

Winged warriors
warn with spear
concealed in rear,
"Stay clear!"

Create paper
to form a shell
where young can dwell
within each cell.

Work hard
feeding grubs
heavy lugs
of beetles, bugs.

Hide their nest
in shrub or tree.
If you should see,
let it be.

Builders Underground

Star-Nosed Mole *Condylura cristata*

The star-nosed mole is named for the ring of twenty-two pink feelers around its snout. A pair of star-nosed moles produces about five young each year. Hairless newborns are helpless at first and depend on their mother's milk. In two weeks their eyes, ears, and star open, and after a month they're independent. Parents can dig through moist soil at several feet per hour and prefer damp places, but they build the nursery high enough in their tunnel to keep it dry. Adults are nearly blind. No other mammal eats faster than a star-nosed mole. Using the feelers in its star to find worms and insects, it snaps up three or four per second.

Black-Tailed Prairie Dog *Cynomys ludovicianus*

Black-tailed prairie dogs are usually noisy and playful, but females will fight if danger threatens their young. Males may have several mates, each with a litter of up to six babies, so they need a lot of room! Instead of climbing trees like their squirrel cousins, these rabbit-size mammals dig systems of burrows called towns that are several feet deep and branch into chambers used as nurseries, bedrooms, and bathrooms. The largest town ever discovered was in Texas. About four hundred million prairie dogs lived there—that's more than the number of people in the United States.

California Trapdoor Spider

Bothriocyrtum Californicum

The trapdoor spider is a master of ambush. It digs a hole big enough to hide in, lines it with silk, and makes a trapdoor with dirt and vegetation to match the ground around it. It attaches the door with a silk hinge, crawls into the hole, and shuts the door. When an unsuspecting small creature creeps too close, the spider leaps out. A male may go out looking for a mate, but a female stays close to home. When her babies hatch, she protects them in the burrow for weeks and feeds them food that she regurgitates from her stomach.

Learn more!

Phillips, Dee. *Prairie Dog's Hideaway*. New York: Bearport, 2012.

Zappa, Marcia. *Star-Nosed Moles*. World's Weirdest Animals. Pinehurst, NC: Big Buddy Books, 2015.

Visit the library or use the internet to find out more about these creatures.

Note: Not every animal in this book has a dedicated reference book for kids. The books listed represent a selection.

Builders on Land

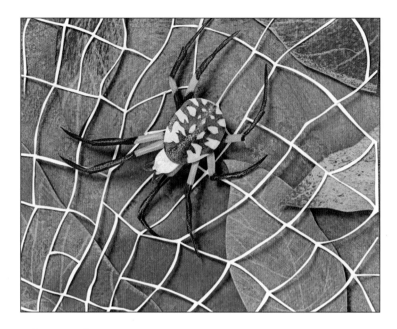

King Cobra *Ophiophagus hannah*
Of the roughly three thousand types of snakes in the world, king cobras are the only ones that make a nest for their eggs and guard them for the first several weeks. Luckily for the babies, the female abandons the nest before they hatch. A king cobra's diet is mostly snakes—and sometimes they eat their own young. King cobras grow longer than any other venomous snake, sometimes reaching up to eighteen feet. They can climb, swim, and crawl, and a king cobra bite can kill an elephant.

Termite *Macrotermes bellicosus*
Some termite mounds are twenty-five feet tall, forty feet around, and as hard as concrete. To build them, worker termites use a combination of their saliva and feces mixed with particles of sand or clay, plus fibers from the wood they chew. Vents inside the mound let air flow in order to hold the temperature steady and protect the nest in the ground below. Hidden in a special chamber, the queen lays up to thirty thousand eggs each day. After the eggs hatch, workers take care of the babies until they are grown, which can take months, depending on climate and other conditions.

Yellow Garden Spider *Argiope aurantia*
These large black-and-yellow spiders spin fragile, complicated webs. The male is smaller and gets only one date. He dies after mating, and the female eats him. Then she lays thousands of eggs and hangs them in silk sacs on her web. At night she may move her eggs to a safe place while she eats her web and reuses the silk to build a new one. She guards her eggs as long as she can, but her days are numbered. She grows frail and dies before her babies hatch.

Learn more!

Sweazey, Davy. *King Cobras*. Amazing Snakes!. Minneapolis: Bellwether Media, 2014.

Markle, Sandra. *Termites: Hardworking Insect Families*. Minneapolis: Lerner, 2007.

Visit the library or use the internet to find out more about these creatures.

Builders in Water

Beaver *Castor canadensis*

Beavers build dams to protect themselves and their families. With chisel-like teeth, they gnaw off tree limbs and cut down trees, drag them into the water to create a dam, and add mud and rocks until the dam forms a pond. Their lodge looks like a mound of sticks, but inside there's a room above water where the family lives. The only entrances are under water, though. Females make a soft nest for their furry newborns. Baby beavers are born with their eyes open and can swim a day later. After nursing for two weeks, they'll chew on wood and eat foliage for the rest of their lives.

Three-Spined Stickleback Fish

Gasterosteus aculeatus

Male sticklebacks take parenting seriously. The male picks a spot in shallow water, hollows out a pit, heaps it with algae or other plant material, adds sand, and glues it all together with sticky goo, called spiggin, from his own body. Swimming back and forth through the pile, he makes a small tunnel to woo a female stickleback to swim through it and lay eggs. The male fertilizes the eggs, chases the female away, and settles down to guard the eggs until they hatch. Then the male protects the babies until they can take care of themselves. Full-service dad!

White-Spotted Pufferfish

Torquigener albomaculosus

To attract a mate, a male pufferfish may work for a week shaping sand and shells into a colorful design on the ocean floor. If it works, a female will lay eggs on it. The male fertilizes and guards the eggs, blowing water over them to keep them healthy. When the eggs hatch, the male leaves the young to fend for themselves. When danger threatens an adult pufferfish, it swallows water and blows up into a ball with venomous spines sticking out in every direction. The pufferfish is one of the deadliest poisonous creatures in the world.

Learn more!

Holland, Mary. *The Beavers' Busy Year*. Mt. Pleasant, SC: Sylvan Dell, 2014.

Visit the library or use the internet to find out more about these creatures.

Builders in Air

Red Ovenbird *Furnarius rufus*

Few creatures work longer to build a nest than red ovenbirds. Sometimes both partners work for months before the mating season to fashion a dome-shaped structure, usually high in a tree. Between snacks of caterpillars, flies, worms, and spiders, they make numerous trips with beak-loads of clay, mud, dung, grass, straw, hair, and other materials until the nest is finally finished and dried rock-hard. They even build a dividing wall inside the nest to protect the nursery after the babies hatch. Both parents take care of their two to four chicks until they're ready to fly. Ovenbirds may mate for life, but they sometimes build a new nest.

White Stork *Ciconia ciconia*

Folklore says that storks bring good luck and deliver babies, but the only babies they deal with hatch from the eggs they lay in enormous nests on rooftops, church spires, and other high places. Some nests are used by many generations of storks and can be seven feet across and ten feet deep. Both parents take care of the chicks until they leave the nest, which happens when they are about two months old. Juveniles aren't very colorful, but adults are nearly four feet tall, with brown eyes, a red bill and legs, a white body, black wing tips, and wings that stretch up to seven feet from tip to tip.

European Paper Wasp *Polistines dominula*

The paper wasp queen hibernates through the winter, but her family dies in the cold. When she wakes, she makes paper for a new nest by chewing dead wood and mixing it with saliva. She places an egg in each six-sided cell in the nest and tucks in a caterpillar for the larva to eat when it hatches. After the larvae are born, she nurtures them until they are ready to turn into male and female wasps. As winter approaches, one or more young females mate so they can be queens next year. All it takes to start a whole colony is one fertilized queen.

Learn more!

Green, Jan. *Incredible Insects: An Amazing Insight into the Lives of Ants, Termites, Bees, and Wasps.* Helotes, TX: Armadillo, 2014.

Visit the library or use the internet to find out more about these creatures.

A Different Kind of Builder

Sun Coral

We're very much alive.
Indeed we have a million mouths to
feed, and each is such a simple
thing—a stomach, tentacles that
sting. And each produces on its
own a chemical that's much like
stone. And over time beyond
belief, we produce a coral
reef, a congregating place to
be for other creatures of the sea.

Sun Coral *Dendrophyllidae tubastraea*

Coral is made up of tiny, tube-shaped animals called polyps.
Male polyps release sperm that fertilize female polyp eggs,
and larvae become new polyps. Cemented together by their
waste—calcium carbonate—groups of polyps form colonies,
and groups of colonies become coral reefs.

LEARN MORE!

Sexton, Colleen. *Coral Reefs*. Learning About the Earth.
Minneapolis: Bellwether Media, 2008.

Visit the library or use the internet to find out more about these creatures.